This Book
Belongs to Jessica

Shrimp cocktail is no longer the only choice on the appetizer menu. Tiny tastes of big flavors from all over the world will make cocktail hour an international affair, and your dinner party a huge success...

now you're cookin'
STARTERS

THIS BOOK JUST MAKES YOU WANNA COOK -

REBO PUBLISHERS

now you're cookin'
STARTERS

Foreword

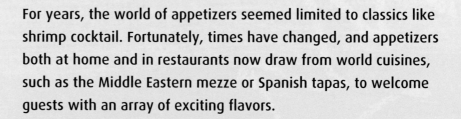

For years, the world of appetizers seemed limited to classics like shrimp cocktail. Fortunately, times have changed, and appetizers both at home and in restaurants now draw from world cuisines, such as the Middle Eastern mezze or Spanish tapas, to welcome guests with an array of exciting flavors.

This collection of appetizers includes creative pre-dinner nibbles, among them Tabbouleh with Grilled Peppers, Mediterranean Spinach and Herb Roulade, and Chicken Yakitori, from kitchens around the globe.

With selections for every palate, season, and desire, you're sure to find the perfect small dishes for everything from a casual family gathering to an elegant party.

U.S. KITCHEN CONVERSION
(LIQUID OR VOLUME, APPROXIMATE)

1 tsp. = 1/3 tbsp./5 ml
1 tbsp. = 1/2 fl. oz./15 ml
2 tbsp. = 1 fl. oz./30 ml
1/4 cup = 2 fl. oz./60 ml
1/3 cup = 2 2/3 fl. oz./79 ml
1/2 cup = 4 fl. oz./118 ml
2/3 cup = 5 1/3 fl. oz./158 ml
3/4 cup = 6 fl. oz./177 ml
7/8 cup = 7 fl. oz./207 ml
1 cup = 8 fl. oz./237 ml

Tabbouleh with Grilled Peppers

Serves 4

PREPARATION

Place the bulgur in a bowl and pour boiling water over to about ½ inch (2 cm) above the level of the bulgur. Leave to soak for 20 minutes. Meanwhile, preheat the broiler to high. Broil the yellow peppers, skin-side up, for 15–20 minutes, until the skin is blistered and blackened all over. Transfer to a plastic bag, seal, and leave to cool. When cold enough to handle, remove and discard the charred skins and roughly chop the flesh.

Blanch the green beans in boiling water for 3–4 minutes. Drain, refresh under cold running water, and set aside. Put the tomatoes into a bowl, cover with boiling water and leave for 30 seconds.
Peel, deseed, and chop.

Combine the ingredients for the dressing and mix well.
Drain the bulgur and transfer to a salad bowl. Add the dressing and toss well. Add the vegetables, green onions, brazil nuts, parsley, and seasoning, and toss together gently to mix.

INGREDIENTS

1 2/3 cups (225 g) bulgur wheat
2 yellow peppers, quartered and deseeded
1/2 lb. (250 g) green beans, halved
2 ripe tomatoes
4 green onions, sliced
2/3 cup (75 g) brazil nuts, chopped roughly
4 tbsp. chopped fresh parsley
sea salt and freshly ground black pepper

FOR THE DRESSING

4 tbsp. extra-virgin olive oil
1 tbsp. whole-grain mustard
1 garlic clove, crushed
1 tsp. balsamic vinegar
1 tsp. white wine vinegar

Salade Niçoise

Serves 6

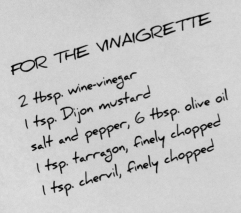

INGREDIENTS

Mixed lettuce, washed and dried
6 1/2 oz. (185 g) canned tuna
3 potatoes, cooked and quartered
2 hard-boiled eggs, quartered
3 tomatoes, quartered
12 black olives, pitted
1/4 lb. (250 g) green beans, blanched
6 anchovy filets, drained
1/2 cucumber, sliced

FOR THE VINAIGRETTE

2 tbsp. wine-vinegar
1 tsp. Dijon mustard
salt and pepper, 6 tbsp. olive oil
1 tsp. tarragon, finely chopped
1 tsp. chervil, finely chopped

PREPARATION

Assemble all the ingredients in a large salad
bowl in the order they are listed.

Dress the salad with the vinaigrette
at the table just before serving.

Celery, Carrot, and Apple Salad with Tahini

Serves 4

PREPARATION

To make the dressing, place the lemon juice, garlic,
tahini paste, and 3 tablespoons of water
in a food processor and blend until smooth.
Alternatively, combine with a fork. Season to taste.

Toss together the carrots, celery heart, and apples and transfer
to individual serving bowls. Drizzle the dressing over.

INGREDIENTS

3 carrots, grated
1 celery heart, thinly sliced
2 red apples, peeled, cored and thinly sliced

FOR THE DRESSING

3 tbsp. lemon juice
1 clove garlic, crushed
2 tbsp. tahini
salt

Beijing Scallion Pancakes

Serves 4 as individual starters

PREPARATION

Beat eggs well. Add scallions, flour, bacon, stock, and salt.
Mix together to form a smooth batter.

Add 2 teaspoons of oil to a 10–inch (25 cm) frying pan on medium heat,
and tilt the pan so that the oil covers it. Pour a quarter of the batter
into the pan, also ensuring it covers the base.

When pancake edge is golden, turn pancake carefully until cooked.
Remove and repeat the procedure 3 more times with extra oil
to yield 4 pancakes.

Serve pancakes hot, cut into slices.

INGREDIENTS

2 eggs
6 scallions, sliced finely
1 1/2 cups (170 g) flour
2 slices bacon, finely chopped
1 cup (8 fl. oz./237 ml) chicken stock
pinch of salt
3 tbsp. vegetable oil

Olive Scones with Thyme-Cured Beef

Makes 24 biscuits or 48 open-faced canapés

PREPARATION

Thyme-Cured Beef: Place sugar, salt, peppercorns, and thyme leaves on a large plate. Roll beef in mixture several times to coat and form a crust. Place beef on a rack set in a shallow dish. Cover. Refrigerate for 24 hours – check from time to time that the crust is still encasing the meat, as the juices that are released during marinating may loosen it.

When ready, using absorbent paper towels, thoroughly wipe away all of the herb crust. Using a very sharp knife, cut beef across the grain into paper-thin slices. (This is easier to do if you place the filet in the freezer for 10 minutes before slicing.) Place slices on a plate. Cover. Refrigerate until ready to use. Olive Scones: Preheat oven to 400°F (200°C). Lightly spray or brush a baking tray with unsaturated oil. Set aside. Sift flour and baking powder together into a large bowl. Add olives, basil, and black pepper to taste. Mix to combine. Make a well in the center. Place milk and mustard in a small bowl, and whisk to combine. Pour into well in flour mixture. Mix quickly to make a soft dough. Turn dough onto a lightly floured surface and knead briefly until smooth.

Press mixture or roll out to form a 1–inch–thick (2 cm) rectangle. Using a 1 ½–inch (3 cm) biscuit cutter, cut out biscuits. Place with sides just touching on prepared baking tray. Bake for 10–12 minutes or until biscuits are well risen and golden. Transfer to a wire rack. Cool slightly. To serve, split biscuits and spread with some chutney. Top with a small mound of beef and a thyme sprig.

INGREDIENTS

chutney of your choice
fresh thyme sprigs

THYME-CURED BEEF

3/4 cup (185 g) sugar
1/2 cup (125 g) salt
3 tbsp. crushed black peppercorns
1 large bunch (50 g) fresh thyme, leaves only
7 oz. (200 g) lean beef filet,
trimmed of visible fat

OLIVE SCONES

1 cup + 3 tbsp. (250 g)
all-purpose flour
2 tsp. baking powder
1/4 cup (45 g) black olives,
rinsed and drained, chopped
1 tbsp. chopped fresh basil
freshly ground black pepper
1 cup (8 fl. oz./250 ml)
buttermilk, 1 tbsp. dijon mustard

Teriyaki Calamari Skewers

Makes 24 small skewers

PREPARATION

Soak 24 small or 8 large bamboo skewers in cold water for at least 20 minutes.

Preheat a barbecue or broiler to a high heat.

Cut each calamari ring in half. Thread strips onto bamboo skewers in an "S" shape, using 1 strip on small skewers and 3 strips on large skewers.

Place skewers on barbecue or under broiler. Cook, turning several times, for 1–2 minutes or until calamari is just cooked.

Teriyaki Sauce: Place shallot, ginger, vinegar, soy sauce, honey, and 1 tablespoon lime juice in a small saucepan over medium heat. Heat. Stir in sesame oil and remaining lime juice. Serve with calamari. If serving as a light meal, accompany with a tossed green salad. The skewers are delicious warm or cold.

INGREDIENTS

2 large calamari (squid) tubes, cleaned, cut into 1/2-inch-thick (1 cm) rings

TERIYAKI SAUCE

1 shallot, thinly sliced
1 tsp. minced fresh ginger
1/4 cup (2 fl. oz./60 ml) rice wine vinegar or sherry
2 tbsp. reduced-salt soy sauce
1 tsp. honey, 2 tbsp. lime or lemon juice
1 tsp. sesame oil

Spinach-Stuffed Pasta Shells with Tomato Sauce

Serves 6

PREPARATION

Preheat the oven to 350ºF (180ºC).
Bring a large pot of salted water to a boil. Add the pasta shells,
boiling until just tender. Drain and allow the pasta shells to cool.

Squeeze the defrosted spinach dry and transfer to a large bowl.
Quickly blanch the baby spinach leaves in hot water, then drain
and add to the frozen spinach. Add the finely chopped red onion, ricotta,
grated Parmesan, fennel, basil, and garlic, and mix thoroughly.
Add salt and pepper to taste.

Heat the olive oil in a deep saucepan and add the chopped spring onions.
Sauté for 2 minutes until softened. Add the chopped tomatoes, sugar,
and salt and pepper to taste. Simmer for 30 minutes,
until the tomatoes have liquefied. Add the dill, stirring thoroughly,
and season with additional salt and pepper, if necessary. Set aside.

Spoon the spinach mixture into the pasta shells, adding just enough
to fill each shell. Set aside. Divide the tomato sauce among six ovenproof
dishes and place five filled pasta shells on top of the sauce in each dish.
Sprinkle with extra Parmesan cheese, cover the dishes with foil,
and bake for 20 minutes. Remove the foil and bake for another
5 minutes, or until golden.

INGREDIENTS

30 jumbo pasta shells
1 lb. (500 g) frozen chopped spinach, thawed
1 large handful of fresh baby spinach leaves
1 small red onion, finely chopped
1 lb. (500 g) ricotta
1 1/3 cups (120 g) grated Parmesan
2 tbsp. fennel seeds
20 fresh basil leaves, chopped
3 garlic cloves, minced
salt and pepper
1 tbsp. olive oil

6 green onions, chopped
3 1/3 lb. (1 1/2 kg) tomatoes
1 tbsp. sugar
salt and lots of freshly ground
black pepper
2 tbsp. dill, chopped
additional Parmesan cheese,
for serving

Toast Strips with Pesto and Ricotta

Serves 6

INGREDIENTS

12 slices artisanal bread, sliced
3 tbsp. olive oil
1/2 lb. (250 g) ricotta
5 tbsp. pesto
black pepper
1/4 cup (25 g) Parmesan

PREPARATION

Toast the bread, and brush with a little olive oil.
Meanwhile, beat together the ricotta and pesto.
Stir in the rest of the olive oil. Season with pepper.

Cut the toast into fingers, discarding the ends.
Spread the ricotta mixture on and shave
Parmesan over, using a vegetable peeler.

Artichokes with Sour-Cream Sauce

Serves 4

INGREDIENTS

4 large globe artichokes
salt
1 1/2 cups (12 fl. oz./355 ml)
sour cream
5 spring onions, finely chopped
1 tbsp. balsamic vinegar
1 clove garlic, finely chopped

PREPARATION

Cut off the artichoke stalks, so that the artichokes stand flat.
Place in a large saucepan of boiling salted water
and simmer, partly covered, for 40 minutes or until tender.
To test if the artichokes are cooked, pull off an outside leaf;
the leaf should come away easily. Remove the artichokes
from the pan and set aside for 30 minutes to cool.

Meanwhile, make the sauce. Mix together the sour cream,
spring onions, balsamic vinegar, and garlic. Pull the central
cone of leaves out of each artichoke, leaving a wall
of leaves around the edge, and discard.
Scrape away the inedible core with a teaspoon,
to leave the edible base.

Spoon plenty of sauce into the artichoke center.
Place the artichokes on plates and eat by plucking
out a leaf and dipping it into the sauce. Use your
teeth to pull away the edible fleshy part at the base
of the leaf, and then discard the rest.

Blinis with Herbed Yogurt Cheese

Makes 20

PREPARATION

Blinis: Place yeast, sugar, and ½ cup (4 fl. oz./125 ml) of the milk in a small bowl.
Let stand for 5 minutes or until frothy. Place flours in a large bowl. Mix to combine.
Make a well in the center, and pour the yeast mixture and remaining milk into the well.
Mix until just combined. Place egg white in a separate, clean bowl. Beat until soft peaks form.
Fold egg mixture into batter. Season with black pepper to taste.
Heat a nonstick frying pan over a medium heat. Lightly spray or brush with unsaturated oil.
Place tablespoons of mixture in pan. (You should be able to cook 5–6 blinis at a time
in a 8- to 12-inch (20–23 cm) frying pan. Cook for 1–2 minutes or until bubbles appear
on the surface. Turn over. Cook second side for 30 seconds or until golden.
Place on paper towels. Keep warm in a low oven while cooking the remaining mixture.
Serve blinis warm or cold topped with a spoonful of Yogurt Cheese
and a lowfat topping of your choice, if desired. (The illustration shows blinis topped
with semi-dried tomatoes.)

YOGURT CHEESE

Line a colander with a double thickness of cheesecloth or muslin.
Place over a large bowl. Add yogurt. Cover with plastic wrap,
and let stand in the refrigerator overnight.
Transfer yogurt to a clean bowl. Discard whey. Add seasonings of your
choice to cheese. Mix to combine. Store cheese in an airtight container
in the refrigerator for up to 1 week. Makes 1 cup (8 fl. oz./250 ml).

INGREDIENTS

1/2 recipe Yogurt Cheese flavored with
1 tbsp. chopped fresh dill
and 1 tbsp. chopped fresh mint

BLINIS

1 tsp. dry yeast, 1 tsp. sugar
11/2 cups (12 fl. oz./355 ml) lowfat milk,
warmed
1 cup (130 g) buckwheat flour
1/2 cup (70 g) all-purpose flour
1 egg white, freshly ground black pepper

YOGURT CHEESE

3 cups (1 lb., 3 1/2 oz./600 g)
plain lowfat yogurt
Seasonings:
chopped fresh herbs
ground spices
chopped fresh chiles
grated vegetables

Stuffed Eggplant Rolls with Parsley Pesto

Serves 6

PREPARATION

Slice each eggplant vertically into six thin slices. Salt lightly and allow the bitter juices to drain for 30 minutes. Rinse briefly and drain well. Slice two large sides off each bell pepper, reserving the remainder for another use. Place the bell-pepper slices under a hot broiler and cook until the skins are blackened. Then place the bell peppers into a plastic bag and seal, allowing them to steam. Set aside for thirty minutes. When cool enough to handle, open the bag and gently peel off and discard the black skins. Allow the peppers to cool.

Heat a grill or cast-iron grill pan and lightly brush or spray the eggplant with oil. Grill the eggplant pieces until golden, and then turn and brush with olive oil. Grill the second side until golden; about 3 minutes each side. Allow to cool. Meanwhile, in a bowl or food processor, combine the feta, ricotta, and herbs with salt and pepper to taste. (If using a processor, take care not to over-process.)

To assemble, lay each eggplant slice on the work surface and top with a large piece of broiled bell pepper. Place a generous spoonful of the cheese filling on top of the pepper (near the bottom end closest to you), and top with 4 arugula or spinach leaves. From the cheese end, roll up firmly but gently, making sure that some of the rocket or spinach protrudes from each end. Serve drizzled with parsley pesto. To make the parsley pesto, pack everything except the oil into a food processor and process. With the motor running, add just enough oil to combine the pesto.

INGREDIENTS
FOR ROLLS

2 large smooth eggplants
6 large red or yellow bell peppers
1-2 tbsp. olive oil
2/3 cup (150 g) feta cheese
1 cup (200 g) ricotta
20 basil leaves
10 mint leaves
1 bunch of arugula (or a handful
of baby spinach)
salt and pepper to taste

FOR PESTO

2 cups Italian flat-leaf parsley
2 cloves garlic
1 tbsp. red wine vinegar
1 tsp. anchovy paste
1/3 cup (2 1/2 fl. oz./75 ml)
olive oil

Vegetable Tempura

Serves 4

INGREDIENTS

2 eggs
1/2 cup (4 fl. oz./125 ml) ice-cold water
1/2 cup (70 g) all-purpose flour, sieved
8 oz. (225 g) jar cranberry and orange sauce, for dipping
vegetable oil, for deep-frying
1 eggplant, cut into thick slices
1 large red onion, cut into wedges
1 1/2 cups (225 g) broccoli, cut into small florets

1 red pepper, deseeded and cut into strips
4 oz. (125 g) green beans, with only one end trimmed
4 oz. (125 g) asparagus, trimmed
sea salt
fresh basil leaves to garnish (optional)

PREPARATION

To make the batter, lightly whisk together the eggs and water. Pour onto the flour all at once and whisk quickly, until the batter is smooth.

Heat the cranberry and orange sauce in a small saucepan, over gentle heat, until warm and runny. Remove from the heat and place in a bowl.

Heat 2 inches (5 cm) of oil in a wok or frying pan. Dip the vegetables in to the batter and coat well. Test the temperature of the oil by dropping in a little batter; if it floats right back to the surface, the oil is hot enough.

Deep-fry the vegetables in small batches for 3–4 minutes or until crisp and golden. Remove with a slotted spoon and drain on paper towels. Season with salt. If using, deep-fry a few basil leaves for 20 seconds, until crisp. Serve the vegetables at once with the dipping sauce.

Celeriac and Herb Remoulade

Serves 4

PREPARATION

Bring a saucepan of water to a boil. Add the eggs and boil
for 10 minutes. Cool under cold running water, remove the shells,
and finely chop the eggs.

Place the celeriac and chopped eggs in a large bowl.
Mix together the olive oil, sesame oil, and lemon juice,
and pour over the celeriac and eggs. Add the parsley,
chives and seasoning. Mix thoroughly.

INGREDIENTS

2 medium eggs
1 lb, 2 oz. (500 g) celeriac, grated
2 tbsp. olive oil
1 tbsp. sesame oil
juice of 1 lemon
3 tbsp. chopped fresh parsley
3 tbsp. snipped fresh chives
salt and black pepper

Mediterranean Spinach and Herb Roulade with Olive Pesto

Serves 8

PREPARATION

Preheat oven to 375°F (190°C).

Butter and line (with parchment paper) a jelly-roll tin and set aside. Wash the spinach several times to remove all grit; then steam or microwave until soft. Squeeze thoroughly to remove all liquid. Chop very finely.

In a mixing bowl, place the spinach, nutmeg, chives, thyme leaves, butter, cream, egg yolks, and Parmesan cheese. Mix thoroughly and season to taste with salt and pepper. Beat the egg whites until firm, and carefully fold into the spinach mixture. Spoon the spinach batter into he prepared tin, smoothing out the edges. Bake for 12–15 minutes, until firm and springy to the touch. Place a clean kitchen towel on a flat surface and place the baked spinach-mixture face-down on the tea-towel. Allow to cool slightly. The steam will help soften the batter, avoiding cracks when it is rolled later.

Meanwhile, make the filling. Finely chop the olives, bell peppers, and tomatoes. Mix all the ingredients except the artichokes in a bowl and season to taste with salt and pepper. If necessary, soften the cream cheese to make it easier to blend. (Do not use a food processor because the vegetables will be too finely puréed.) Remove the baked spinach mixture from the tin. Remove the paper. Trim any tough edges from the spinach. Spread with the cheese mixture and dot with the finely sliced artichokes. From the long edge, roll up the spinach and filling, using the tea-towel to help you. Once rolled, wrap the roulade in the tea-towel and chill for at least 6 hours.

To make the pesto, pit all the olives, and blend in a food processor with the basil leaves, breadcrumbs, and enough olive oil to correct the consistency. To serve, allow the roulade to come to room temperature and slice into 1–inch–thick (2 cm) portions. Serve with a spoonful of the Kalamata pesto on the side.

INGREDIENTS

FOR ROULADE

1 lb. (450 g) spinach, 1/4 tsp. nutmeg
1 bunch chives, finely chopped
1 tsp. fresh thyme leaves, chopped
2 tbsp. butter
3 tbsp. double cream, 2 large eggs, separated
3 tbsp. grated Parmesan cheese
salt and pepper to taste

FOR FILLING

1/2 cup (50 g) Kalamata olives
1/2 cup (50 g) sun-dried bell peppers

1/2 cup (120 g) sun-dried tomatoes
3/4 cup (180 g) cream cheese
2 tbsp. sour cream
20 basil leaves, sliced
2 roasted artichokes, sliced
salt and pepper to taste

FOR PESTO

2 1/2 cups (300 g) Kalamata olives
1 bunch of basil
2 tbsp. breadcrumbs, olive oil

Fava Bean Eggah

Serves 4

INGREDIENTS

1 onion, finely sliced
1/4 tsp. pepper
2 tbsp. olive oil
1/4 tsp. salt
6 eggs
tsp. cumin
2 cups (350 g) fava beans, cooked
2 tbsp. chopped basil or cilantro

PREPARATION

Sauté the onion in 1 tablespoon
of the oil until it begins to brown.

Beat the eggs in a bowl and add the fava beans,
onion, pepper, salt, cumin, and basil or cilantro.
Mix well.

Heat the remaining oil in an omelet pan,
and pour in the egg mixture.
Turn the heat to low and cook for about 15 minutes.

Either flip over as for frittata or place
under a broiler to cook the top.

NOTE
"Eggah" is an Arabic term for a hearty omelet.

Baked Ricotta Mushrooms

Makes 10

INGREDIENTS

10 mushrooms, stems removed
1 tbsp. grated Parmesan
1 tbsp. dried breadcrumbs

RICOTTA AND HERB FILLING

1/2 cup (125 g) reduced-fat ricotta cheese
3 sun-dried tomatoes, soaked in warm water until soft, chopped

1 tbsp. finely diced red onion
1 tbsp. chopped fresh basil
1 tbsp. snipped fresh chives
1 tsp. lemon juice
freshly ground black pepper

PREPARATION

Preheat oven to 350ºF (180ºC). Line a baking tray with nonstick baking paper. Set aside.

Filling: Place ricotta, tomatoes, onion, basil, chives, lemon juice, and black pepper to taste in a bowl. Mix to combine.

Spoon filling into mushrooms. Place on prepared baking tray. Combine Parmesan cheese and breadcrumbs. Sprinkle over mushrooms. Bake for 10–15 minutes or until filling is set and golden.

Mushroom and Cranberry Tart

Serves 6

INGREDIENTS

12 oz. (350 g) pie-crust pastry, defrosted if frozen

2 tbsp. sesame oil

1 bunch of spring onions, chopped

9 oz. (250 g) large mushrooms, finely sliced

4 oz. (125 g) oyster mushrooms, broken into large chunks

2/3 cup (5 fl. oz./150 ml) dry white wine

1 cup (100 g) cranberries, defrosted if frozen, 1/2 lb. (280 g) tofu

1/2 cup (4 fl. oz./125 ml) lowfat milk

2 medium eggs, lightly beaten

3 tbsp. snipped fresh chives

zest and juice of 1/2 a lemon

salt and black pepper

PREPARATION

Preheat the oven to 425°F (220°C). Roll out the pastry and use it to line a 10-inch (25 cm) tart dish. Line with baking or parchment paper, fill with pie weights, and cook for 15 minutes. Remove the paper and beans, and cook for another 5–10 minutes until golden. Set aside. Reduce the temperature to 375°F (190°C).

Meanwhile, heat the oil in a wok or large, heavy-bottomed frying pan. Add the spring onions and stir-fry for 2–3 minutes, until they start to brown. Add the large open and oyster mushrooms and stir-fry for 3 minutes or until they begin to soften.

Pour in the wine and simmer for 6–8 minutes, until reduced slightly. Add all but a handful of the cranberries and boil for 1–2 minutes, until most of the liquid has evaporated and the cranberries start to pop.

Using a hand blender or food processor, blend the tofu, milk, and eggs to a smooth purée. Add the chives, lemon zest, lemon juice, and seasoning, and mix well. Spoon the mushroom mixture into the pie crust and pour the tofu purée over. Scatter with the remaining cranberries. Cook for 35 minutes or until golden and firm.

Wild Mushroom Palmiers with Herb Mayonnaise

Makes 40 palmiers

PREPARATION

Preheat oven to 425°F (220°C). Heat the butter and oil in a large frying pan, and sauté the minced garlic and finely chopped onion. Meanwhile, finely chop the mushrooms in a food processor. Add these to the onion mixture and cook gently for 5 minutes. Sprinkle the flour over the mushroom mixture and stir to incorporate. Add the water or stock and stir until the mixture thickens and boils. Allow to cool thoroughly before adding the chopped chives and basil.

Lay a sheet of pastry on a flat surface. Spread one-sixth of the cooled mushroom mixture over the pastry and sprinkle with one-sixth of the finely chopped nuts. Fold opposite sides of the pastry in to meet in the middle, and then fold again so that the pastry looks like a compact log. Lay the log on its side and gently press down firmly. Slice the mushroom-filled log into 8 slices and place slices on a greased baking sheet. Repeat with remaining pastry and filling ingredients. Freeze the uncooked pastry for five minutes; then bake for 12–15 minutes or until golden brown. To make the herb mayonnaise, mix the herbs and mayonnaise together and allow the flavors to blend for at least 30 minutes. Season with salt and pepper, and serve with the pastries.

NOTE

These pastries freeze well (both unbaked and baked), and can be made days or weeks ahead. Defrost, bake, or reheat before serving.

INGREDIENTS

1 tbsp. butter
1 tbsp. olive oil
2 cloves garlic, minced
1 onion, finely chopped
7 oz. (200 g) wild mushrooms
(such as Swiss brown, porcini, shiitake)
1 tbsp. flour
2 tbsp. water/stock
1/4 cup (5 g) chives, finely chopped
1/4 cup (5 g) basil, finely chopped
6 sheets puff pastry

1/4 cup (30 g) pistachio nuts, toasted and finely chopped

FOR THE HERB MAYONNAISE

2 tbsp. cilantro, finely chopped
2 tbsp. chives, finely chopped
1 tbsp. parsley, finely chopped
1/2 cup (4 fl. oz./125 ml)
mayonnaise
salt and pepper to taste

Butternut-Squash Ravioli with Sun-Dried Tomatoes

42

PREPARATION

Cook or microwave the squash until just tender. Drain well and mash. (For this recipe, the squash needs to be fairly dry.)

Stir the Parmesan cheese into the hot squash, add salt and pepper, and leave the mixture to cool.

To make the ravioli, arrange four wonton wrappers on a board, brush edges lightly with the egg, and place one heaped teaspoon of squash on each wrapper. Top each with a second wrapper, pressing the edges firmly together to secure. Cut the ravioli into circles using a 3-inch (7 ½ cm) cookie cutter. Repeat this process until all the squash is used.

Bring a large pan of salted water to a boil and cook the ravioli for about 2–3 minutes, until al dente. Remove very carefully with a slotted spoon and drain. (Ravioli should be cooked in several batches.)

Place the oil in a clean pan, add the ravioli, dried tomatoes, and basil and swirl the pan very gently until the ravioli is coated with oil. Serve immediately.

INGREDIENTS

1 lb. (500 g) butternut squash
1 egg, beaten
1/4 cup (30 g) grated Parmesan cheese
3 tbsp. virgin olive oil
salt and pepper
12–18 sun-dried tomatoes
8 oz. (250 g) packet wonton wrappers
2 tbsp. chopped basil

Creamy Chickpea and Tomato Dip

Serves 6

PREPARATION

Soak the chickpeas in cold water for 12 hours, or overnight.
Drain and rinse thoroughly, place in a saucepan, and cover with fresh water. Bring to a boil and cook for 10 minutes, removing any foam with a slotted spoon. Reduce the heat and simmer, covered, for 1 hour or until tender.

Drain the chickpeas, reserving 6 tablespoons of the cooking liquid, and set a few aside to garnish. Blend the remaining chickpeas to a fairly smooth purée with the reserved cooking liquid, the oil, and lemon juice in a food processor. Transfer to a bowl.

Place the tomatoes in a bowl and cover with boiling water.
Leave for 30 seconds, then peel, deseed, and chop. Add the tomatoes to the chickpea purée with the garlic, lemon zest, spring onions (if using), parsley or mint, and seasoning.

Mix well and refrigerate for 30 minutes. Before serving, garnish with the reserved chickpeas and drizzle with olive oil, if desired.

INGREDIENTS

1/2 lb. (250 g) dried chickpeas

6 tbsp. olive oil, plus extra for drizzling (optional)

zest of 1/2 a lemon and juice of 2 lemons

12 oz. (350 g) plum tomatoes

2 cloves garlic, crushed

2 spring onions, finely chopped (optional)

3 tbsp. finely chopped fresh parsley or mint

salt and black pepper

Terrine of Leek and Roasted Bell Peppers with Tomato Vinaigrette

Serves 8–10

PREPARATION

Seed the bell peppers and cut into large slices. Place these under a hot broiler and cook until the skins are blackened. Place the black bell peppers into a plastic bag and seal, allowing them to steam. Set aside for thirty minutes. Remove the peppers from the bag and remove the skins. Set aside. Slice the leek(s) lengthways and separate the leaves. Wash in cold water to remove all the grit, and then plunge the largest cleaned leaves into a pot of boiling water. Boil for 3 minutes, then remove the leek and rinse under cold water. Reserve the remaining leek for the garnish. Line a standard loaf pan with plastic wrap. Drape the cooked leek leaves over the base and sides of the pan, allowing the long ends to hang over the sides. Heat the butter and sauté the spring onions until softened. Mix the softened cream cheese, goat cheese, herbs, spring onion mixture, and salt and pepper in the large bowl of an electric mixture. Sprinkle the gelatin over the cold water and allow to soak for 1 minute. Place the gelatin mixture in the microwave and heat for 20 seconds on medium until the mixture is boiling, watching carefully to prevent boiling over. Stir well with a fork. Add the dissolved gelatin and cream to the cheese mixture and mix to combine. Pour one-third of the cheese mixture into the prepared loaf pan and cover with alternate red and yellow bell-pepper slices. Cover with another third of the cheese mixture, repeating the bell-pepper layer. Finish with remainder of cheese mixture, and drape the leek overhang back over the cheese filling to enclose. (Use any leftover leek to fill in the gaps, if necessary.) Chill overnight. Cut the remaining leek into very fine strips, and deep-fry them in hot oil (about 350°F/180°C) until golden. Drain the leeks on paper towels and store in an airtight container. Remove the terrine from the loaf tin and discard the cling wrap. Using an electric knife, slice thick, even portions of the terrine and serve accompanied by the vinaigrette. To make the vinaigrette, whisk the vinegar, olive oil, mustard, and sugar together until emulsified. Finely chop the tomato, cucumber, and olives, and mix together. Sprinkle the chopped vegetables around each slice of terrine on each individual plate and drizzle the vinaigrette over. Top with a tangle of deep-fried leeks.

INGREDIENTS

2 red bell peppers, 2 yellow bell peppers
1 large leek (or 2 medium leeks)
3 1/2 tbsp. butter
1 bunch spring onions
2/3 cup (150 g) cream cheese
1 1/4 cups (300 g) soft goat cheese
1/2 cup (10 g) Italian flat-leaf parsley, chopped
20 fresh basil leaves, torn
salt and pepper to taste
2 tsp. gelatin, 1 tbsp. cold water
1 cup (8 fl. oz./300 ml) double cream

VINAIGRETTE

3 tbsp. white wine vinegar
3 tbsp. olive oil
1/2 tsp. French mustard
1/2 tsp. sugar
1 large tomato, seeded
1 medium cucumber, seeded
10 Kalamata olives, pitted
oil (for frying)

Caramelized Shallot and Asparagus Toast

Serves 6

PREPARATION

Heat the oil in a wok or large, heavy-bottomed frying pan.
Add the shallots, garlic, and chile (if using), and stir-fry for 4–5 minutes,
until they start to brown. Add the sugar and the soy sauce and stir-fry
for 3–4 minutes, until the shallots are evenly browned.

Add the vinegar and wine to the shallots and bring to a boil.
Reduce the heat and simmer, uncovered, for 8 minutes or until the
shallots have softened and the liquid has thickened and looks glossy.
Add the asparagus, cover, and cook for 4–5 minutes, until tender,
stirring occasionally.

Place the tomatoes in a bowl and cover with boiling water.
Leave for 30 seconds, and then peel, deseed, and chop. Add to
the asparagus with the lemon juice. Stir and heat for 1–2 minutes.

Meanwhile, preheat the broiler to high. Broil the bread on both sides.
Serve the toast slices topped with the vegetable mixture and garnished
with the parsley or cilantro.

INGREDIENTS

3 tbsp. olive oil
1 1/2 cups (300 g) shallots, thickly sliced
2 cloves garlic, thickly sliced
1 red chili, deseeded and sliced (optional)
1/2 tbsp. brown sugar
2 tbsp. dark soy sauce
1 tbsp. white wine vinegar or cider vinegar
2/3 cup (5 fl. oz./150 ml) white wine
1 cup (100 g) asparagus tips

4 plum tomatoes
juice of half a lemon
12 thick slices French bread
flat-leaf parsley or cilantro,
to garnish

Vegetable Toast with Tomato Dressing

50

PREPARATION

Place the eggplants, carrots, and red peppers in a bowl and season well.

Toast the bread for 3 minutes each side or until golden brown.
Meanwhile, for the dressing, place the tomatoes in a bowl of boiling
water for 30 seconds; then peel, deseed, and finely chop.

Heat the sunflower oil in a large frying pan over high heat.
Cook the vegetables for 4 minutes, stirring, until they have softened
and are just tender. Remove and set aside.

In the same pan, heat the olive oil and add the spring onions and white
wine vinegar. Cook, stirring occasionally, for 1–2 minutes, until hot,
and then stir in the tomatoes. Pile the vegetables on top of the toasts,
drizzle with the hot dressing, and serve.

INGREDIENTS

2 eggplants, sliced thinly lengthwise

2 carrots, sliced thinly lengthwise

2 red bell peppers, deseeded and thinly sliced

sea salt and freshly ground black pepper

4 thick slices rustic white bread

1 tbsp. sunflower oil

2 tomatoes

4 tbsp. extra-virgin olive oil

2 spring onions, sliced

1 tbsp. white wine vinegar

NOTE

When slicing the eggplants and carrots, try using a vegetable peeler or mandoline to make long ribbons.

Skordalia (Potato-Garlic Dip)

Serves 6

PREPARATION

Peel the potatoes, cut into cubes, and boil until tender.
Drain and mash.

Crush garlic in a press or in a mortar with a pestle.
Add the salt, and then combine with mashed potatoes.
(A creamier consistency will be obtained if the mixture
is transferred to a food processor at this stage.)

While mixing or beating the potatoes, add the olive oil gradually,
followed by the lemon juice and pepper.

Serve as a dip. Or heat and serve as a side dish to a main meal.

INGREDIENTS

2 lb. (1 kg) potatoes
5 or more garlic cloves
1 tsp. salt
1/2 cup (4 fl. oz./125 ml) olive oil
juice of half a lemon
pepper

Hummus

Serves 4-6

PREPARATION

Cook the chickpeas in water for about 1 ¼ hours or until tender. Drain. Put all the ingredients except paprika and parsley into a food processor. Blend to a creamy paste. Serve on a plate dusted with paprika and garnished with parsley.

INGREDIENTS

1 cup (150 g) chickpeas (garbanzo beans), soaked

1 tsp. salt

2 tbsp. olive oil

4 tbsp. tahini

1 tsp. cumin seeds

juice of 2 lemons

1 tsp. paprika

4 garlic cloves, crushed

parsley sprigs, to garnish

Carrot and Potato Dip

PREPARATION

Boil the carrots, potatoes, and salt in water until the vegetables are soft.
Drain and blend in a food processor with the garlic, cumin,
chili pepper, and lemon juice.
Gradually add the oil and blend to a smooth, thick consistency.

NOTE
Serve this spicy dip with fresh crusty bread or pita bread.

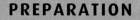

INGREDIENTS

1 1/2 lb. (750 g) carrots, chopped
1 lb. (500 g) potatoes, peeled and chopped
1/2 tsp. salt
3 garlic cloves, chopped
4 tsp. cumin seeds
1 chili pepper, chopped
2 tbsp. lemon juice
3 tbsp. olive oil

Yogurt Cheese Balls in Olive Oil and Herbs

INGREDIENTS

4 pints (4 quarts/2 1/4 l) plain yogurt
2 tsp. salt
finely chopped mint, marjoram,
and tarragon
paprika
olive oil

PREPARATION

Line a colander or two large sieves with scalded muslin or cheesecloth and place over receptacle bowls to catch drainage.

Whisk the salt into the yogurt and pour into the colander or sieves. Leave to drain overnight; it will become a soft, creamy curd.

Mold the curd into small rounds, place them on a perforated dish, and leave them in the refrigerator for 24 hours.

The cheeses can be eaten immediately, sprinkled with the chopped herbs or paprika and served on slices of tomato. If you want to keep them, leave them in the refrigerator for another 2–4 days, (depending on how creamy you want them to be), and then pack them into jars and cover with olive oil. Store in a cool place.

Provençal Anchovy Dip

PREPARATION

PROVENÇAL ANCHOVY DIP

Place the anchovy filets and garlic in a bowl or mortar and grind to a pulp.
Add the oil, lemon juice, mayonnaise, and cream. Mix well and season to taste with pepper.
Transfer to a decorative serving bowl and sprinkle with paprika. Chill until ready to serve.

HOMEMADE MAYONNAISE

Place the eggs and the dry ingredients in a food processor or blender and blend
for 5 seconds. Then, with the machine still running, very gradually
add the oil in a thin, steady stream until the mixture is thick and creamy.
Add the vinegar and lemon juice and blend once more.

NOTE 1

The strong flavors of anchovies and garlic combine in this dish to make
an ideal accompaniment to raw vegetables or bread.

NOTE 2

The secret of making mayonnaise is not to use cold ingredients;
remove eggs from the refrigerator a few hours before use.
The ingredients must be beaten constantly, and, if the mixture curdles,
immediately add a few drops of cold water.

INGREDIENTS

1/3 cup (30 g) canned anchovy filets,
drained
1 garlic clove, chopped roughly
3 tbsp. oil
1 tsp. lemon juice
1/4 cup (2 fl. oz./60 ml) mayonnaise
1/4 cup (2 fl. oz./60 ml) cream
1/4 tsp. pepper
1/2 tsp. paprika

HOMEMADE MAYONNAISE

2 eggs at room temperature
1 tsp. dry mustard powder
1 tsp. salt, 1 tsp. superfine
sugar
1/4 tsp. cayenne
1 cup (8 fl. oz./250 ml) oil
1 tbsp. white vinegar
1 tbsp. lemon juice
Makes 1 1/2 cups
(12 fl. oz./375 ml)

Carpaccio with Mustard Mayonnaise

PREPARATION

Trim meat of all visible fat and cut into wafer-thin slices.
Arrange beef slices, lettuce leaves, and watercress attractively
on four serving plates. Sprinkle with Parmesan cheese.

To make the mustard mayonnaise, place egg, lemon juice, garlic,
and mustard in a food processor or blender and process to combine.
With machine running, slowly add oil and continue processing
until mayonnaise thickens. Season to taste with black pepper.
Spoon a little mayonnaise over salad and serve immediately.

INGREDIENTS

1 lb. (500 g) beef filet, in one piece
1 head lettuce, leaves separated and washed
1 bunch (250 g) watercress
1 cup (90 g) Parmesan cheese, grated

MUSTARD MAYONNAISE

1 egg, 1 tbsp. lemon juice
2 cloves garlic, crushed
2 tsp. Dijon mustard
1/2 cup (4 fl. oz./125 ml) olive oil
freshly ground black pepper

NOTE

To slice beef very thinly,
wrap the filet in plastic wrap
and place in the freezer
for 15 minutes or until firm.
Slice using a very sharp knife.

Fruity
Pork Roulade

PREPARATION

To make filling, place first nine ingredients in a food processor
and process until finely chopped.

Open steaks and pound to about ¼ inch (5 mm) thick. Spread filling over
steaks and roll up tightly. Secure each roll with string.

Place stock, celery, and onions in a large saucepan and bring to a boil.
Add pork rolls. Cover and simmer for 20 minutes or until pork is cooked.
Transfer pork rolls to a plate and set aside to cool. Cover and refrigerate
for 2–3 hours. To serve, cut each roll into slices.

INGREDIENTS

2/3 cup (60 g) pine nuts
1 cup (100 g) pitted prunes
2/3 cup (60 g) dried apricots
1 tbsp. grated fresh ginger
1 tsp. chopped fresh sage
3 tbsp. fruit chutney
4 strips bacon, chopped
3 tbsp. brandy
freshly ground black pepper, to taste

4 lean butterflied pork steaks
2 cups (16 fl. oz./500 ml)
beef stock
4 stalks celery, chopped
2 onions, chopped

Spicy Chicken Wings with Orange Pieces

Serves 4

66

PREPARATION

Place the chicken wings in a shallow, non-metallic dish and pour the sauce over. Squeeze the juice from 1 orange and pour into the empty sauce bottle. Give it a shake to release all the sauce, and then pour the juice over the chicken. Turn the chicken to coat well. Cover and place in the fridge to marinate for 10 minutes.

Preheat the broiler to high. Place the chicken wings in a single layer on a large baking sheet and pour the marinade over, reserving a little for basting. Broil the wings for 20 minutes, turning frequently and basting with the reserved marinade, until the flesh is cooked through and the skin is charred.

Meanwhile, peel the remaining oranges and divide into segments. Divide the salad leaves between 4 plates, add the orange segments and spring onions, and top with the hot chicken wings.

INGREDIENTS

12 chicken wings
1 1/4 cup (10 fl. oz./300 ml) hoisin sauce or barbecue sauce
3 oranges
4 cups (130 g) mixed greens
3 spring onions, sliced

Breadsticks Wrapped with Parma Ham and Arugula

Serves 6

INGREDIENTS

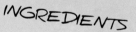

1 cup (15 g) arugula
or basil leaves
3 tbsp. olive oil
6 thin slices Parma ham
6 breadsticks

PREPARATION

Brush the arugula or basil with a little of the oil.
Put a few leaves in the middle of each ham slice,
and then place a breadstick in the center, leaving
about 3 inches (7 ½ cm) uncovered, to use as a grip.

Tightly wrap the ham around the breadstick, tucking
it in neatly at the top.
Brush the ham with the rest of the oil.

Vietnamese Spring Rolls with Homemade Peanut Sauce

PREPARATION

Soak the cellophane noodles in a bowl of hot water to cover for 5–10 minutes until tender. Drain immediately and rinse with cold water to halt the cooking. Cut noodles with scissors to a manageable length and toss with vinegar, fish sauce, crushed peanuts, and shrimp. Mix fresh herbs together and set aside. Finely shred the cabbage leaves and slice the spring onions into fine julienne. In a large bowl, mix together the herbs, both kinds of cabbage leaves, spring onions, noodle mixture, and grated carrot, tossing thoroughly.

Working with 1 wrapper at a time, soak the rice wrapper in warm water for 30 seconds and lay on a flat surface. On each wrapper, place a small amount of the mixed vegetable-noodle filling. Roll up tightly, folding the sides in, to enclose the filling. Continue rolling and folding until all ingredients are used.

To make the peanut sauce, heat the oil and sauté the garlic and minced chili until softened, about 2 minutes. Add all remaining ingredients and whisk while heating. Bring to a boil and simmer until thickened slightly, about 3 minutes.

To serve, slice each roll on the diagonal, and rest one half over the other. Serve the sauce separately in a small pot for dipping.

NOTE

Since these wrappers do fry successfully, you might want to serve half of them fresh and half of them fried.

INGREDIENTS

1 1/2 oz. (50 g) package cellophane noodles
3 tbsp. rice vinegar, 1 tbsp. fish sauce
4 tbsp. roasted peanuts, crushed
12 large shrimp, cooked and finely chopped
20 Thai basil leaves, finely sliced
10 Asian mint leaves, finely sliced
1/4 bunch fresh cilantro, finely chopped
4 leaves of Chinese cabbage (bok choy)
2 cabbage leaves, finely shredded
5 spring onions, 1 medium carrot, finely shredded
12–16 rice paper wrappers (8 inches/20 cm diameter)

FOR SAUCE

2 tbsp. peanut oil
5 cloves garlic, minced
1/2 small red chili pepper, minced
5 tbsp. peanut butter
1 1/2 tbsp. tomato paste
3 tbsp. hoisin sauce, 1 tsp. sugar
1 tsp. fish sauce
3/4 cup (6 fl. oz./175 ml) water
1/4 cup (40 g) peanuts, crushed

Pork Skewers with Artichoke Salsa

PREPARATION

Place pork, breadcrumbs, onion, garlic, oregano, cumin, chili powder, and egg in a bowl. Mix to combine.

Shape tablespoons of pork mixture into balls, and place on a plate lined with plastic food wrap. Cover and refrigerate for 30 minutes.

Preheat barbecue or broiler to medium heat. Thread four balls onto a lightly oiled skewer. Repeat with remaining balls. Place skewers on lightly oiled barbecue grill or broiling pan and cook, turning frequently, for 8 minutes or until cooked through.

To make salsa, heat oil in a frying pan over medium heat. Add onion and cook, stirring, for 3 minutes or until onion is golden.

Add artichokes, tomatoes, tomato paste, and oregano and cook, stirring, for 3–4 minutes longer or until heated through. Serve with pork skewers.

INGREDIENTS

1 lb. (500 g) lean ground pork
1 cup (60 g) breadcrumbs, made from stale bread
1 onion, chopped
2 cloves garlic, crushed
1 tbsp. chopped oregano
1 tsp. ground cumin
1/2 tsp. chili powder
1 egg, lightly beaten

ARTICHOKE SALSA

1 tbsp. olive oil
1 onion, chopped
1 cup (185 g) marinated artichoke hearts, chopped
4 tomatoes, seeded and chopped
2 tbsp. tomato paste
1 tbsp. chopped fresh oregano

Pâté Maison

Serves 4

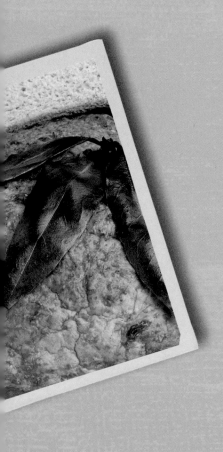

PREPARATION

Preheat the oven to 400°F (200°C).

In a blender, food grinder, or processor (using the steel knife blade), mix the chicken, veal, garlic, and shallot until fine. Add the remaining ingredients except the bay leaves and process everything until the mixture is smooth and the ham finely chopped. Place in a tureen with the bay leaves on top and bake for 40 minutes or until the pâté pulls away from the sides and is brown on top.

Cover and refrigerate when cool. Serve with crusty French bread.

INGREDIENTS

10 oz. (315 g) mixed raw chicken
and veal pieces
1 garlic clove, cut in half
1 shallot, cut in half
3 strips raw bacon, chopped
6 slices Parma ham, chopped
1 egg
1 tbsp. brandy
a pinch each of salt, pepper, and cinnamon
3 bay leaves

Chicken Satay

PREPARATION

THAI MARINADE

A spicy marinade for satay sticks. Serve with the peanut sauce recipe that follows.
Accompany with vegetable crudités and steamed rice.
Put all ingredients into a food processor and blend to a smooth paste.
Marinate beef, pork, lamb, or chicken for at least 2 hours. Thread onto skewers and grill or broil.

PEANUT SAUCE FOR SATAY

Preheat oven to 375°F (190°C). Place peanuts in a pan and roast for 15 minutes.
This will also loosen the skins. Remove from the oven and rub skins off the peanuts.
Grind the peanuts in a food processor.
Put onion in a pan with the oil and cook until it is clear. Add garlic and chilis.
Simmer and stir in the water, ground peanuts, cayenne, sugar, and salt.
When the sauce is smooth, stir in the soy sauce and lemon juice.
Keep refrigerated, with a layer of oil on top to seal. It will keep for weeks.

NOTE 1

You can make a larger quantity and keep it refrigerated in a sealed jar.

NOTE 2

Serve this delicious sauce with satays or to accompany vegetable
crudités. Although there will be a difference in flavor, you can
substitute peanut butter for roasted and ground peanuts.

INGREDIENTS

1 tsp. Thai curry paste
3 garlic cloves, chopped
1 tbsp. soy sauce
1 tbsp. chopped lemon grass
1/2 cup (4 fl. oz./125 ml) coconut milk

PEANUT SAUCE FOR SATAY

2 1/3 cup (315 g) raw shelled peanuts
1 small onion, thinly sliced
1 tbsp. oil

3 garlic cloves, chopped
3 chiles
1 cup (8 fl. oz./250 ml)
water
1/4 tsp. cayenne
1/2 tsp. superfine sugar
1/2 tsp. salt
1 tbsp. soy sauce
1 tbsp. lemon juice

Potted Chicken and Ham

Serves 4

INGREDIENTS

3/4 cup (170 g) butter + 3 tbsp.

2 cups (200 g) cooked skinless chicken or turkey pieces

1 cup (100 g) cooked ham pieces

black pepper

1/4 tsp. ground nutmeg

pinch of allspice

pinch of cayenne pepper

4 fresh bay leaves

PREPARATION

To clarify the butter, place it in a small saucepan and melt over low heat for 3–4 minutes, taking care not to let it brown. Line a sieve with damp muslin, place over a bowl and pour the butter into the sieve, discarding the milky deposit left in the pan. Leave the strained liquid (clarified butter) to cool for 5–10 minutes.

Meanwhile, blend the chicken or turkey and the ham until fairly smooth in a food processor. Add the pepper, nutmeg, allspice, and cayenne to taste and blend until combined. Gradually pour in just under three-quarters of the clarified butter, blending all the time until mixed.

Spoon the mixture into small dishes or ramekins and top each with a bay leaf. Pour over the remaining butter to seal, then refrigerate for 2–3 hours, or overnight.

Chicken Yakitori

Serve immediately as finger food

PREPARATION

Place chicken in a glass bowl. Mix marinade ingredients together
and pour over chicken. Cover and place in refrigerator
to marinate for several hours or overnight.

Thread 2 tenderloins onto each skewer, using a weaving motion.
Heat barbecue or electric grill to medium-high.
Grease grill bars or plate lightly with oil.

Place skewers in a row and cook for 2 minutes on each side,
brushing with marinade as they cook and when turned.
Remove to a large plate.

INGREDIENTS

1 lb. (500 g) chicken tenderloins

MARINADE

1/4 cup (2 fl. oz./60 ml) teriyaki sauce
1/4 cup (2 fl. oz./60 ml) honey
1 clove garlic, crushed
1/4 tsp. ground ginger
small bamboo skewers, soaked
oil for greasing

Chicken and Almond Triangles

Makes 20 triangles

PREPARATION

Heat olive oil in a frying pan and sauté the almonds until pale gold. Quickly remove with a slotted spoon and drain on paper towels.

Add onion and fry until soft; stir in salt and spices and cook until aromatic. Add ground chicken and stir-fry until almost cooked. Add chopped tomatoes, raisins, parsley, almonds, and wine and simmer, covered, for 15 minutes. Uncover and cook until juices are absorbed. Allow to cool. Thaw the pastry according to package instructions. Remove 14 sheets. (Repack and refreeze remainder.)

Position pastry with long side parallel to work edge in front of you. Cut into 3 even 6–inch–wide (15 ½ cm) strips. Stack and cover with a clean tea towel. Take 2 strips at a time, spray each lightly with canola oil spray, and fold in half, long side to long side. Spray surface with oil spray.

Preheat oven to 350°F (180°C). Place a teaspoon of filling on bottom end of each strip. Fold right-hand corner over to form a triangle, and then fold on the straight, and then on diagonal until end is reached. Repeat with remaining. Place on a tray sprayed with oil. Spray tops of triangles with oil and bake for 20–25 minutes. Serve hot.

INGREDIENTS

1 tbsp. olive oil
1/2 cup (60 g) slivered almonds
1 medium onion, finely chopped
1/2 tsp. salt, 1 tsp. ground cinnamon
1 tsp. paprika
2 tsp. ground cumin
1 lb. (500 g) ground chicken
2 small tomatoes, chopped
1/4 cup (45 g) raisins, chopped
2 tbsp. finely chopped flat-leafed parsley

1/4 cup (2 fl. oz./60 ml) dry white wine
1 packet filo dough
canola oil spray

VARIATIONS

1/2 lb. (250 g) chicken stir-fried with 1 chopped onion, cooled and mixed into 1/2 lb. (250 g) ricotta and 1 beaten egg

Curried Chicken Rolls

Makes 16–20 pieces

PREPARATION

Heat oil in a small pan. Add onion and garlic and fry until
onion is soft. Stir in curry paste and cook for a minute.
Add lemon juice and stir to mix. Set aside.

Combine the ground chicken, breadcrumbs, salt, pepper,
and cilantro, and add the onion-curry mixture. Mix well.
Place a thawed sheet of puff pastry on the work surface
and cut in half across the center.
Pile half of the ground-chicken mixture in a thick ½–inch–wide
(1 ½ cm) strip along the center of the strip.

Preheat the oven to 370°F (190°C).
Brush the exposed pastry at the back with water. Lift the front strip
of pastry over the filling and roll to rest on the back strip. Press lightly
to seal. Cut the roll into 4 or 5 equal portions. Repeat with the second
half of the ground-chicken mixture and then with a second sheet.
Glaze with milk and sprinkle with sesame seeds. Place onto a flat baking
tray. Bake for 10 minutes, reduce heat to 350°F (180°C), and continue
cooking for 15 minutes, or until golden brown. Serve hot.

INGREDIENTS

2 tsp. canola oil

1 medium onion, finely chopped

1 small clove garlic, crushed

2 tsp. mild curry paste

1 1/2 tbsp. lemon juice

1 lb. (500 g) ground chicken

3 tbsp. dried breadcrumbs

1/2 tsp. salt

1/2 tsp. pepper

2 tbsp. chopped fresh cilantro

2 sheets frozen puff pastry

1 tbsp. milk, to glaze

1 tbsp. sesame seeds

NOTE

May be made in advance and reheated in a moderate oven.

Fresh Salmon Spring Rolls with Herb Dipping Sauce

Makes 12

PREPARATION

To make the marinade: Whisk together the rice vinegar, lime juice, chopped cilantro, and ginger. Cut the salmon filet into finger-sized pieces, each about 3 inch x 1 inch (8 x 2 cm). (You should have 12 pieces.) Place these into the marinade and marinate for 30 minutes.

To make the dipping sauce: While the salmon marinates, whisk together, in a small bowl, the lime juice, rice vinegar, soy sauce, fish sauce, sugar, ginger, cilantro, and parsley. (Alternatively, for a smoother sauce, process all these ingredients briefly until the herbs are finely chopped.) Set aside.

Meanwhile, cut the spring onions into 3–inch (8 cm) lengths. Finely slice the lengths into thin strips. Peel the carrot, cut into 3–inch (8 cm) lengths, and then julienne the carrot. Remove the salmon from marinade and pat dry.

Fill a large bowl with warm water and soak the rice-paper wrappers, one at a time, until softened. When one wrapper is soft, place it on a clean tea towel and place a piece of salmon on top. Add some strips of spring onion, carrot, and cilantro leaves, and then roll up the filling tightly, folding the sides in as you roll.

Place the rolled-up spring roll on the seam and repeat the soaking, rolling, and folding until all the ingredients have been used.

To cook the salmon rolls, heat some peanut oil to a depth of ½ inch (2 cm). Fry the rolls, seam-side down, until golden underneath; turn and cook the other side.

Drain on paper towels, and then serve immediately with the dipping sauce.

INGREDIENTS
FOR SALMON

1/4 cup (2 fl. oz./60 ml) seasoned rice vinegar

1/4 cup (2 fl. oz./60 ml) fresh lime juice

2 tbsp. chopped fresh cilantro

1 tsp. ginger root, peeled and grated

1 lb. (500 g) salmon, skin removed

4 spring onions, 1 carrot

12 rice-paper wrappers

1/2 bunch fresh cilantro

peanut oil, for frying

FOR SAUCE

3 tbsp. lime juice

2 tbsp. rice vinegar

1 tbsp. soy sauce

1 tbsp. fish sauce

2 tsp. sugar

2 tsp. fresh ginger, grated

1/2 cup fresh cilantro

2 tbsp. fresh parsley

Gravlax Spirals

Makes 20 pieces

INGREDIENTS

1/2 cup (125 g) reduced-fat ricotta cheese, 3 tbsp. chopped fresh dill, 1/2 cup (100 g) plain lowfat yogurt

2 slices lavash bread (or 2 tortillas)

1/4 cup (2 fl. oz./60 ml) honey mustard

3 1/2 oz. (100 g) gravlax, smoked salmon, or smoked ocean trout

lemon juice

freshly ground black pepper

PREPARATION

Place ricotta cheese, dill, and yogurt in bowl. Mix to combine. Set aside.

Spread lavash bread or tortillas with mustard. Top with salmon. Spread with ricotta mixture, leaving 4 inches (10 cm) uncovered at one short end. Sprinkle with lemon juice and black pepper to taste.

Starting at the covered short end, roll up firmly. Wrap in plastic food wrap. Refrigerate for several hours or until ready to serve.

To serve, cut rolls into 1-inch-thick (2 cm) slices. Arrange attractively on a serving platter.

Smoked Fish Tart

Serves 6

TO MAKE THE TART
Preheat the oven to 375°F (190°C). Line a pie dish with the pastry
and chill for 30 minutes. Place the flaked fish in the pie shell.
Put the rest of the ingredients into a bowl and whisk them together.
Pour this mixture over the fish. Bake the tart for 30–40 minutes.

TO MAKE THE CRUST
Sift the flour and salt into a bowl.

Cut the butter into small pieces and add to the bowl.
Rub the butter into the flour with your fingertips until the butter
is completely absorbed and the texture resembles breadcrumbs.

Mix the egg yolk with the water and lemon juice.
Make a well in the flour, add the liquid, and mix together with
your fingertips to form a ball. Add more moisture if it gets too dry.

Put the dough on a floured surface and knead it lightly with the palms
of your hands until smooth. Wrap in plastic wrap and chill for 30 minutes
or up to 3 days. Put the dough on a floured surface and roll it out with
a floured rolling pin. Line the pie dish and chill before filling and baking.

INGREDIENTS

1 pie crust (see recipe, left)
1/4 cup (30 g) Parmesan cheese
2 cups (225 g) cooked and flaked
    smoked fish
salt and pepper
3/4 cup (6 fl. oz./175 ml) heavy cream
1 tsp. fennel seeds
3 egg yolks, beaten

FOR THE CRUST

1 1/4 cups (200 g) flour, sifted

2 tsp. iced water
1/4 tsp. salt
lemon juice
1/2 cup (125 g) butter
1 egg yolk
egg wash (beaten egg yolk)

NOTE

This dish can be made with
any type of smoked fish, such
as haddock, cod, or trout.

Sesame Shrimp Triangles with Chili Sauce

Serves 4

PREPARATION

Blend shrimp, garlic, egg, cornstarch, oil, and soy sauce to a paste in a food processor. Alternatively, grind shrimp with a pestle and mortar, and mix with the other ingredients.

Spread one side of each slice of bread evenly with shrimp paste. Sprinkle with sesame seeds, remove crusts, and cut into 4 triangles. To make dipping sauce, mix together ginger, chili sauce, and lime juice. Set aside.

Heat 1 inch (2 ½ cm) of oil in a large frying pan over medium to high heat. Add half the shrimp triangles, shrimp-side down, and fry for 4–5 minutes on each side, until deep golden. Drain on paper towels and keep warm while cooking the remaining prawn triangles. Serve with dipping sauce.

INGREDIENTS

4 oz. (115 g) cooked peeled shrimp,
defrosted if frozen
1 clove garlic, chopped
2 tbsp. beaten egg
1 tsp. cornstarch
1/2 tsp. sesame oil
a few drops of light soy sauce
3 slices white bread
2 tbsp. sesame seeds
groundnut oil, for deep-frying

DIPPING SAUCE

1/2-inch (1 cm) piece fresh ginger,
finely chopped
2 tbsp. hot chili sauce
juice of half a lime

Grilled Sardines with Orange and Dill Relish

Serves 6

PREPARATION

Slash the sardines diagonally 3 or 4 times on each side, using a sharp knife. Mix together the oil, orange zest, and seasoning. Add the sardines and turn to coat. Cover and place in the fridge for 30 minutes.

Meanwhile, make the relish. Slice the top and bottom off each orange with a sharp knife, then cut off the skin and pith, following the curve of the fruit. Cut between the membranes to release the segments, and chop into ½-inch (1 cm) pieces. Mix with the spring onions, chiles, dill, capers, and oil.

Preheat the grill or broiler to high. Put the sardines onto the grill rack or broiling pan, reserving the marinade. Grill or broil for 3 minutes on each side, brushing occasionally with the marinade, or until the flesh has turned opaque and the skin has browned. Garnish with dill and serve with the relish.

INGREDIENTS

12 fresh sardines, scaled and gutted
3 tbsp. olive oil
zest of 1 orange
salt and black pepper

FOR THE DILL RELISH

4 large oranges
1 bunch of spring onions, finely sliced
1–2 red chilis, deseeded and finely chopped
3 tbsp. chopped dill, plus extra to garnish

2 tbsp. capers, rinsed
and drained
1–2 tbsp. extra-virgin olive oil

Index